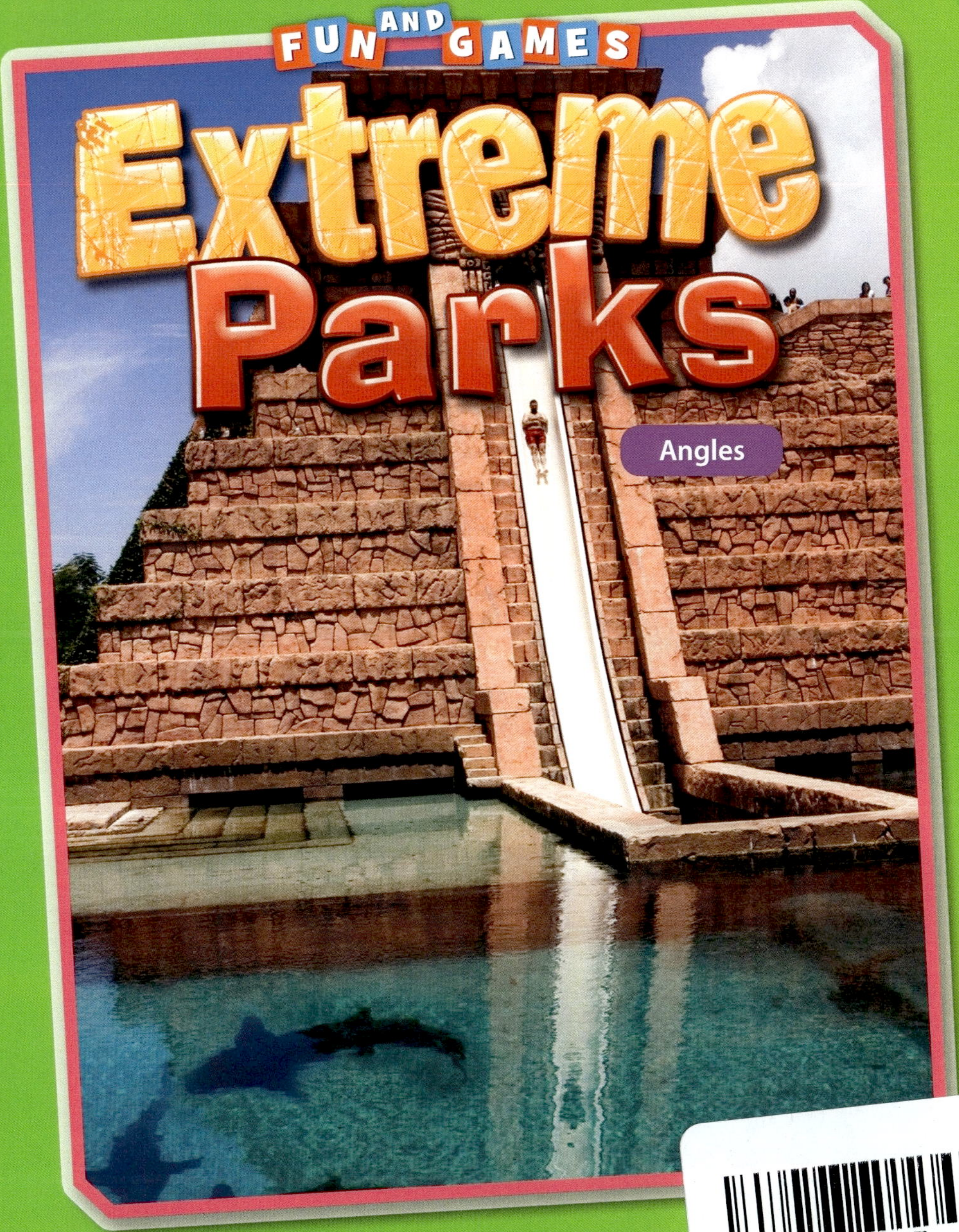

Cathleen D’Alessandro, M

Consultants

Michele Ogden, Ed.D
Principal
Irvine Unified School District

Colleen Pollitt, M.A.Ed.
Math Support Teacher
Howard County Public Schools

Publishing Credits

Rachelle Cracchiolo, M.S.Ed., *Publisher*
Conni Medina, M.A.Ed., *Managing Editor*
Dona Herweck Rice, *Series Developer*
Emily R. Smith, M.A.Ed., *Series Developer*
Diana Kenney, M.A.Ed., NBCT, *Content Director*
Stacy Monsman, M.A., *Editor*
Kevin Panter, *Graphic Designer*

Image Credits: Cover and p.1 Shane Pinder/Alamy Stock Photo; pp.6–7, 9 (inset), 11 (inset), 15 (top inset) Timothy J. Bradley; p.9 manwithacamera.com.au/Alamy Stock Photo; p.10 (bottom) Brian Caissie/Getty Images; p.13 Dani Tot/Alamy Stock Photo; p.14 (top) Chris Rabior/Alamy Stock Photo; p.15 (bottom back) Raul Arboleda/AFP/Getty Images, (bottom front) Chris Hyde/Getty Images; pp.18–19 Ian Dagnall/Alamy Stock Photo; pp.20–21 John Seaton Callahan/Getty Images; p.22 (bottom) Niels Poulsen DK/Alamy Stock Photo; p.23 Peter Forsberg/People/Alamy Stock Photo; pp.24–25 Chris Batson/Alamy Stock Photo; p.25 (inset) age fotostock/Alamy Stock Photo; p.31 Brian Caissie/Getty Images; all other images from iStock and/or Shutterstock.

Teacher Created Materials
5301 Oceanus Drive
Huntington Beach, CA 92649-1030
http://www.tcmpub.com

ISBN 978-1-4258-5562-8

Table of Contents

Extreme Parks 4

Skate Parks 6

BMX Parks 12

Water Parks 18

Amusement Parks 22

Future Parks 26

Problem Solving 28

Glossary 30

Index 31

Answer Key 32

Extreme Parks

Imagine that you are at the top of a 40-story roller coaster. You're about to experience a free-fall drop. Your heart is pounding out of your chest. You grip the metal bar tighter and close your eyes. You take a deep breath, and then…it happens. Your jaw drops. You try to scream, but nothing comes out. In a matter of seconds, the coaster comes to a stop, and you open your eyes. You just had the most terrifying experience of your life. Would you do it again? Chances are, you will!

All around the world, people seek thrilling adventures. Some people look to extreme sports for a bit of danger. Others prefer to **plunge** down a colossal water slide or ride a twisting roller coaster. People are always finding ways to push their limits. They want to go faster and reach new heights. Where do people go for these adrenaline-pumping experiences? Welcome to the world of extreme parks!

Passengers plunge down a 50-foot drop at Six Flags Discovery Kingdom in Vallejo, California.

Riders start their plummet down a 40-meter vertical drop at Efteling theme park in the Netherlands.

Skate Parks

When skateboarding became popular, skate parks began to pop up in cities around the world. Before skate parks were built, **skaters** took their tricks to the streets. This was not safe. Skaters were injured because of uneven street surfaces and collisions with cars. Now, skaters can go to skate parks to practice their tricks.

Every skate park has unique features. Some parks are designed to **mimic** street and sidewalk conditions. Other parks have bowl-like structures with smooth, curved concrete. Skaters can do **aerial** tricks off a **half-pipe**. They can pick up speed to do 180 **ollies**. Or, they can invent new tricks of their own.

Skateboarding has become a five billion dollar industry in the United States. It is so popular that there are now skateboarding competitions. The X Games draws huge crowds. Skaters can compete in many events. Some contests are to see who can do the best trick. Others are to see who can get "the most air" off a **ramp**.

LET'S EXPLORE MATH

To do a 180 ollie, skaters must pop into the air and do a half rotation. When skaters land, they and their boards are facing the opposite direction.

1. What is the name of a 180-degree angle?
2. Max is learning to do a 180 ollie, but right now he can only make half the rotation. How many degrees does he rotate? What is the name of this type of angle? Make a sketch to show your thinking.
3. What number do you think skaters use to describe ollies that are full rotations? Why?

This diagram shows a skater doing a 180 ollie.

The X Games skateboarding competitions are held twice a year at skate parks all around the world. Most of these skate parks are built and then torn down after the event. Before the start of the X Games, the skate park must be designed and built. Designers and builders work with skaters to make sure every course is built just right.

Some of the best skaters in the world compete at the X Games. One event they compete in is the half-pipe. This is a ramp that curves up at both ends. At the top, skaters perform high-flying tricks.

One of the most famous X Games athletes is Tony Hawk. He is a skateboarder from San Diego, California. He started skating when he was only 9 years old. By the age of 20, he was known as the best in the world for his ramp tricks. He won more than 70 contests. He even won gold medals at the 1995 and 1997 X Games. Now, he helps build skate parks that are free to the public in low-income areas all around the United States.

Tony Hawk gets "big air" on the half pipe at a festival in Australia.

LET'S EXPLORE MATH

Look at the illustration of a skateboarder doing a noseslide trick. The skater is sliding the nose edge of the board along a rail.

1. What is the measurement of the angle shown in the illustration? What is the name of this type of angle?
2. Sketch the angle. Draw a ray dividing the angle in half. What is the measurement of each of the two angles formed? What is the name of this type of angle?

Skate parks have evolved over time. The first skate parks were built in the 1970s. The design looked similar to swimming pools and ditches. Skaters had to pay to use these parks. Today, most skate parks are free. They include both "street" designs and traditional elements, like half-pipes, bowls, and pools.

Like skate parks, the design of **skateboards** changed as well. The first skateboard was made by nailing wheels to a fruit crate. When surfing became popular, skateboards took the shape of a small surfboard. There was just one problem—there was no way to brake. So, a **kicktail** was added to the back of the board. This let riders to do more tricks. Of course, they could also brake more easily.

The wheels changed, too. At first, skateboard wheels were made of metal. But, they were heavy. This made it hard to jump. To lighten the wheels, clay was used. This didn't work, either. When riders landed, the wheels sometimes cracked. Then, a plastic material was used to make the wheels. These wheels were softer and provided better traction. Skateboarding would never be the same!

Venice Beach skate park in California

LET'S EXPLORE MATH

Look at the angle shown in the illustration.

1. What is the name of this type of angle? How do you know?
2. Use a protractor to measure the angle. Be sure to line up the straightedge of the protractor with the horizontal ray of the angle.
3. Does the degree measure of the angle support your reasoning in problem 1?

BMX Parks

Similar to skate parks, **BMX** parks have become more popular over the years. *BMX* means "bicycle motocross," or "bike racing." BMX riders ride BMX bikes, which are smaller and lighter than other bikes. This makes them perfect for racing. Riders can go to BMX parks to learn new tricks and practice old skills.

BMX racing parks are designed and built to include racetracks and ramps. The racetracks are built in open spaces. They are designed with three levels. There are beginner, intermediate, and expert tracks. The more advanced tracks have steeper **slopes**. The steeper the slope, the more air riders get over the ramps.

BMX racing has come a long way. Now, riders can compete in racing events starting at age five! It has become so popular that it is now an Olympic sport. It made its debut in 2008 in Beijing, China. Both men and women compete in the events.

Francisco Sousa competes in a BMX racing event in Portugal in 2013.

BMX riders race at Olympic Park in London, England.

BMX rider Nina Buitrago "gets some air" off a ramp.

Just like skate parks, BMX parks must be designed and built prior to an X Games competition. The courses are designed so that riders can perform tricks on half pipes and street courses. Most of the athletes who compete are male. But, that's starting to change. More and more female athletes are joining the sport.

Nina Buitrago (bih-TRAH-goh) has broken barriers for women in BMX riding. She is one of the most well-known female BMX riders today. Buitrago has been riding for over 15 years. She started a website and a magazine to showcase women riders. She wants to see more women in BMX riding in the future.

LET'S EXPLORE MATH

Look at the angle shown in the illustration of the BMX racer.

1. What is the name of this type of angle? Explain your reasoning.
2. Use a protractor to measure the angle.
3. Does the degree measure of the angle support your reasoning in problem 1?

Caroline Buchanan is another female BMX rider. The Australian is known as the "Queen of Dirt." She has won over 20 BMX titles and is a two-time Olympian in the sport. She also competes in mountain bike riding events. Buchanan wants to help other female riders make progress. She funds and mentors an all-girls BMX team.

Caroline Buchanan competes in a time trial race.

A BMX rider performs a tail whip.

It didn't take long for BMX parks to become popular. Just like skaters, BMX Freestyle riders began by doing their tricks in the streets. It all started in the early 1970s in California. BMX riders did tricks in empty swimming pools and parking lots. They raced each other and jumped off ramps. They used curbs and stairs as ramps to "get some air." Now, BMX riders can go to BMX parks. Also, some skate parks allow BMX riders safe spaces to perform tricks. They can also go to BMX racing parks. The dirt tracks are similar to motocross, or motorcycle racing.

Just like skateboards, the parts of BMX bikes have changed over time. Frames were made lighter. This way riders could go faster and catch more air. The handlebars were built so that they could rotate in a full circle, or 360 degrees. Pegs were added to the front and back wheels so that riders could do more tricks. And, unlike skateboards, BMX bikes have brakes. Sometimes, racers remove the front brake to make a bike even lighter. To ride at top speed, every little bit helps!

Visitors coast down a funnel slide at a water park in Australia.

Water Parks

Extreme parks are not just for sports. A trip to a water park can also be a thrill. Most water parks are built outdoors, but some are built indoors. They include swimming pools, water coasters, and slides. There are over 1,200 water parks in the United States today. Over 85 million people visit water parks each year.

Water parks began to spring up at lakes and campsites in the late 1960s. These first water parks only had a few slides. The first large-scale water park in the United States was built in Orlando, Florida. George Millay opened Wet 'n Wild in 1977. He is now known as the Father of the Water Park. Wet 'n Wild was open for almost 40 years. Visitors had lots of thrill rides to choose from. They could free fall down a water slide. They could dive into 4-foot (1-meter) waves in a large **wave pool**. Or, they could float on a tube along a lazy river.

Wet 'n Wild in Orlando, Florida

Designers and engineers must work together to build safe rides for water parks. To build a water slide, designers will first plan and sketch a drawing of the slide. Then, engineers make a model of the slide. Lastly, they build the actual slide. The water slide must go through many test runs to make sure it is safe before people ride it.

An engineer and construction workers build a tube slide at a water park in Russia.

A surfer rides a wave at Seagaia OceanDome wave pool in Miyazaki, Japan.

Besides water slides, designers and engineers also build wave pools. Wave pools must create constant waves, similar to how wind blows real waves in an ocean. Sometimes, **pistons** are used to make waves. Short discs within tubes move up and down, sending out blasts of air. This creates waves. The waves gradually move toward the shallow end of the pool. In a wave pool, people can splash and jump their way through waves. Or, they can ride a wave on a surfboard just like they are in the ocean!

Amusement Parks

For the extreme thrill seeker, an amusement park is the place to go. People have been going to these parks for hundreds of years. The world's oldest amusement park is in Denmark. Bakken opened in 1583. It is still running today! Over 2 million people visit the park every year.

This park is known for its setting as well as its age. Bakken means "The Hill." But, its full name means "Deer Park Hill." Bakken is found in the middle of a large forest. There are trees dating back over 400 years. More than 1,000 deer roam free. Most visitors want to enjoy the view of the forest. So, many get to Bakken by foot, bike, or horse and carriage.

Like most amusement parks, Bakken has rides, games, shows, and of course, roller coasters! Bakken's first roller coaster was built in 1932. Before being updated in 2010, this wooden coaster ran with a brakeman. The brakeman sat in the rear of the train and controlled the speed of the coaster. This is much different than the computers used today.

Riders enjoy the bumper cars at Bakken in Denmark.

Visitors enjoy a snack underneath Bakken's wooden coaster.

About 290 million people flock to amusement parks to ride roller coasters each year. Roller coasters can be made from wood or steel. Wooden roller coasters were the first type of coasters ever built. But, wood has its limits. Now, more coasters are made of steel. Steel roller coasters are much taller and faster than wooden coasters. They have steeper hills with heart-stopping drops. They have higher loops that turn 360 degrees. At the top of loops, riders hang upside down.

Roller coasters have also become safer over time. Just like building water coasters, designers and engineers work together to build safe roller coasters. After they make a design, they are ready to build the coaster. They must decide where to place the tracks. They need to be sure the weights and speeds are set just right. Their measurements have to be exact to make the coaster safe for riders. Many test runs are needed before people ride the roller coaster. But once complete, riders can hop on for the rides of their lives!

LET'S EXPLORE MATH

Look at the angle shown in the photo. The Formula Rossa passenger car and the pole form an angle. This angle is decomposed into two parts. If the whole angle measures 70 degrees, what is the value of m? Prove your answer.

People ride Formula Rossa, the fastest roller coaster in the world, at Ferrari World in Abu Dhabi, United Arab Emirates.

Future Parks

What a great time to be a thrill seeker! There are so many extreme parks to visit. There are skate parks and BMX parks where people can perform tricks and compete for awards. There are water parks where they can surf or plunge down water slides. People can also visit amusement parks to brave roller coasters that climb to dizzying heights.

Extreme parks have evolved over time. Skateboard and BMX parks allow for daring tricks. Water rides and roller coasters have become taller and faster. Imagine what extreme parks might look like in years to come. Engineers have the chance to create parks that have never been imagined. You never know. Maybe your ideas will come to life in the future!

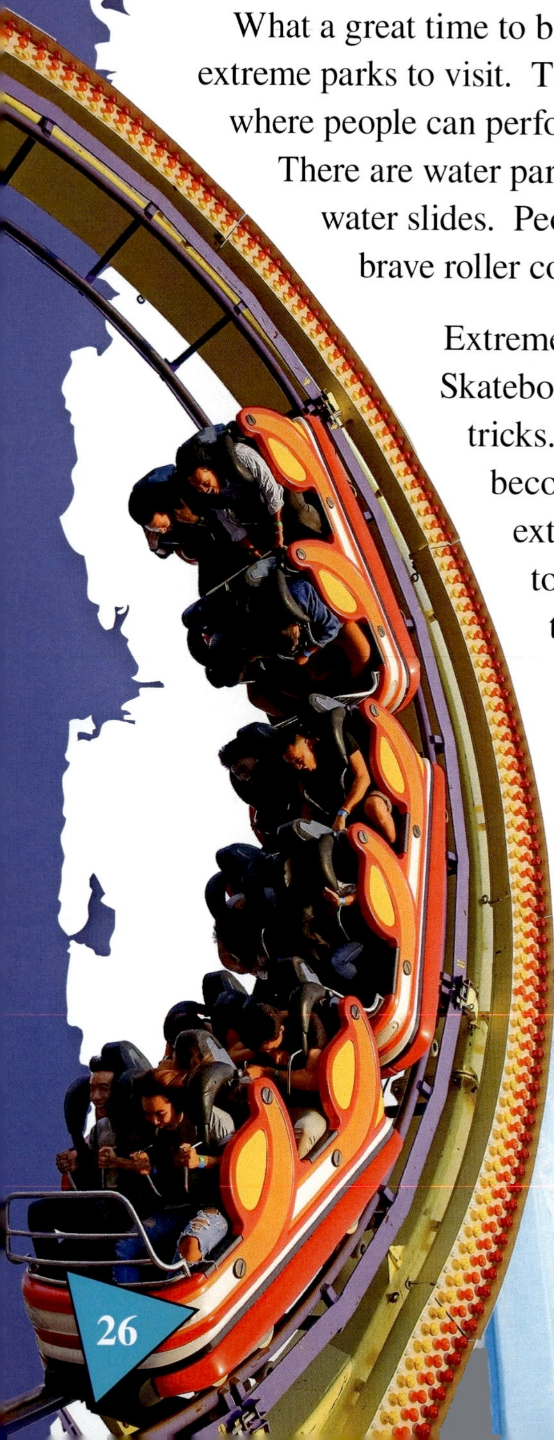

skyride in Vienna, Austria

Problem Solving

Now, it is your turn to design an extreme park. What type of park will you create? Will it be used for sports, water rides, or roller coasters? Do you have a unique idea of your own?

Use graph paper to sketch your park. Be sure to include at least one of each of the following angles. Remember, you can always include more than what is listed here.

- right angle
- straight angle
- acute angle
- obtuse angle

1. Use a protractor to measure and label the acute and obtuse angles in your design.
2. Using the vertex as an end point, draw a ray to decompose the right angle in your design into two parts. Use a protractor to measure one of the two angles. How can you find the other angle measure? Explain your thinking.
3. Using the vertex as an end point, draw two rays to decompose the straight angle in your design into three parts. Use a protractor to measure two of the three angles. How can you find the missing angle measure? Show your thinking to prove your answer.

Glossary

aerial—something done in the air

BMX—Bicycle Motocross

half-pipe—curved ramp that is used for doing tricks on a skateboard or bike

kicktail—upward bent tips on a skateboard deck

mimic—to imitate

ollies—tricks in which skaters push down the tail of the board while jumping to bring the board off the ground

pistons—short discs within a tube that move up and down

plunge—to fall or dive into water

ramp—sloping surface made out of cement, wood, or dirt

skateboards—small, narrow boards with wheels on both ends

skaters—people who skateboard

slopes—surfaces that have a downward or upward slant

wave pool—large pool that makes waves similar to those in an ocean

Index

amusement park, 22, 24, 26

Bakken, 22–23

BMX, 12–17, 26

brakeman, 22

Buchanan, Caroline, 15

Buitrago, Nina, 14

engineers, 20–21, 24, 26

Formula Rossa, 25

Hawk, Tony, 8–9

Millay, George, 19

skate park, 6, 8, 10, 12, 14, 17, 26

Sousa, Francisco, 13

water park, 18–21

Wet 'n Wild, 18–20, 26

X Games, 6, 8, 14

Answer Key

Let's Explore Math

page 7:

1. Straight angle
2. 90°; right angle
3. 360; Explanations will vary, but should include that a half rotation is 180° and a full rotation can be found by doubling 180° to get 360° (180° + 180° = 360°).

page 9:

1. 90°; right angle
2. 45°; acute angles

page 11:

1. Acute angle; An acute angle measures more than 0° but less than 90°.
2. 30°
3. Yes, the angle measurement indicates that the angle is acute.

page 15:

1. Obtuse angle; An obtuse angle measures more than 90° but less than 180°.
2. 140°
3. Yes, the angle measurement indicates that the angle is obtuse.

page 25:

25°; 70 – 45 = 25

Problem Solving

Designs will vary, but should include at least one of each of the angles listed.

1. Answers will vary, but should include one angle that measures less than 90° and one greater than 90°.
2. Answers will vary, but should show a right angle decomposed into two acute angles. The missing angle measure can be found by using a protractor or subtracting the known angle measure from 90.
3. Answers will vary, but should show a straight angle decomposed into three angles. The missing angle measure can be found by using a protractor or subtracting the sum of the known angle measures from 180.